the information store

CHALLENGING MINDS. INSPIRING SUCCESS.

CITY COLLEGE
NORWICH

Please return on or before the last
date stamped below.
Contact: 01603 773 114 or
01603 773 224

0 9 FEB 2018

A FINE WILL BE CHARGED FOR OVERDUE ITEMS

THE REAL DEAL
ILLNESS

Terri DeGezelle

www.heinemann.co.uk/library

Visit our website to find out more information about Heinemann Library books.

To order:

☎ Phone 44 (0) 1865 888066

📄 Send a fax to 44 (0) 1865 314091

💻 Visit the Raintree bookshop at www.heinemann.co.uk/library to browse our catalogue and order online.

Heinemann Library is an imprint of **Pearson Education Limited**, a company incorporated in England and Wales having its registered office at Edinburgh Gate, Harlow, Essex, CM20 2JE – Registered company number: 00872828

Heinemann is a registered trademark of Pearson Education Ltd.

Text © Pearson Education Limited 2009
First published in hardback in 2009
The moral rights of the proprietor have been asserted.

Edited by Kristen Truhlar, Rachel Howells, and Louise Galpine
Designed by Richard Parker and Manhattan Design
Picture research by Mica Brancic
Production: Victoria Fitzgerald

Originated by Chroma Graphics (Overseas) Pte. Ltd
Printed and bound in China by Leo Paper Group.

ISBN 978 0 431 90807 6 (hardback)
13 12 11 10 09
10 9 8 7 6 5 4 3 2 1

British Library Cataloguing in Publication Data
DeGezelle, Terri, 1955-
Illness. - (The real deal)
155.9'16

A full catalogue record for this book is available from the British Library.

Acknowledgements
We would like to thank the following for permission to reproduce photographs: ©Alamy pp. **25** (Photofusion Picture Library); ©Bubbles pp. **7**; ©Corbis pp. **4** (Falko Updarp/Zefa), **13** (Robert Landau), **26** (Stefanie Grewel/Zefa); ©Getty Images pp. **6** (Stone); ©Jupiter Images p. **21** (Thinkstock Images); ©Masterfile pp. **11** (Russell Monk), **12** (Kathleen Finlay), **15** (Rory Ooms), **17** (Brian Kuhlmann), **27**; ©PunchStock pp. **5** (Rubberball), **10** (Polka Dot Images), **22** (SuperStock/Blend Images), **23**, **24** (Blend); ©Rex Features pp. **14** (Sipa Press), **19** (Alix/Phanie); ©SuperStock pp. **8** (Dynamic Graphics Value), **9** (Age Fotostock), **16** (Image Source), **20** (Creatas), **18**.

Cover photograph of an ECG machine reproduced with permission of ©iStockphoto (angelhell); cover photograph of a skeleton reproduced with permission of ©iStockphoto (vadkoz).

We would like to thank Anne E. Pezalla for her invaluable help in the preparation of this book.

Every effort has been made to contact copyright holders of any material reproduced in this book. Any omissions will be rectified in subsequent printings if notice is given to the publishers.

Contents

Some words are printed in bold, **like this**. You can find out what they mean by looking in the glossary.

What is illness?

Illness is when the body is not functioning the way it was meant to. Often illness means not feeling well. A person can be ill for many different reasons. There are many types of illness. Some illnesses last a short time, but others can last a lifetime.

Having an illness is difficult for the people who are ill, as well as their family and friends. Having an illness can make it difficult to go about normal activities. Some illnesses require people to change their lifestyle and eating patterns. Sometimes people feel sad when they are ill, because for some people it is hard to be happy when they don't feel well.

The common cold is an illness that almost everyone catches at some point.

Common illnesses

A common illness is an illness that many people get. Conjunctivitis is an example of a common illness. A person with conjunctivitis has an eye that is red, itchy, and puffy. A cold is another common illness. A cold may include a cough, runny nose, or sore throat. Many people get colds each year. Both conjunctivitis and a cold usually get better in a short amount of time.

Serious illnesses

A major illness is more serious. **Heart disease** is a major illness. It affects adults more often than young people. People with heart disease cannot spread it to another person. **Cancer** is another major illness. People of any age can become ill with cancer. Cancer is an illness that people cannot catch or give to one another.

A long-term or major illness could mean a stay in hospital.

NEWSFLASH

In the past, not much was known about what caused illness or how to help people get better. Today scientists and doctors are learning more about what makes people sick. Natural products, made from plants, are becoming more popular to help treat illnesses. In the last 25 years, more than 70 percent of all new medicines have come from natural sources.

Different types of illness

Contagious

Illnesses can be contagious or non-contagious. Contagious illnesses can be passed on by normal day-to-day contact among people, through coughing, sneezing, or shaking hands. **Viruses** cause many contagious illnesses.

People with contagious illnesses can spread **germs** to others before they even know they are sick. This is one reason why contagious illnesses are so hard to stop from spreading. One example of a contagious illness is influenza (also called flu). Cases of the flu can spread very quickly through a family or an entire school. Often with an illness caused by a virus, people go to see a doctor. They follow the doctor's orders and feel better within a few days.

NEWSFLASH

The influenza virus can live for 72 hours on the surface of telephones and desktops.

It is rare for a person to catch the same type of flu twice because their body wins the fight against the virus within a few weeks.

Sometimes when people learn a person has a contagious illness, they become afraid because they don't know how to protect themselves from getting sick. Some people can feel **isolated** when they have a contagious illness.

Washing hands can help prevent contagious illnesses from spreading.

Non-contagious

Some illnesses are non-contagious. People with non-contagious illnesses cannot spread their illnesses to other people.

Cystic fibrosis and **asthma** are two examples of illnesses that can't be spread to other people. These illnesses can't be passed on to other people because germs are not the cause of them. Cancer is another non-contagious illness.

People who live or go to school with people who have non-contagious illnesses don't need to worry about catching the illness. It is not possible to catch a non-contagious illness by spending time with a person who has this type of illness.

Asthma is not contagious. People with asthma may need to use an **inhaler** to help them breathe.

Chronic illnesses

A long-term illness is also known as a **chronic** illness. A chronic illness doesn't go away. People with a chronic illness are sick with the same disease for a very long time – maybe even the rest of their lives.

Some chronic illnesses, such as **cerebral palsy** and **arthritis**, make it difficult for people to do physical activity, such as walk, run, or participate in certain sports. Other chronic illnesses, such as **Crohn's disease** and **diabetes**, make it difficult for people to eat certain foods.

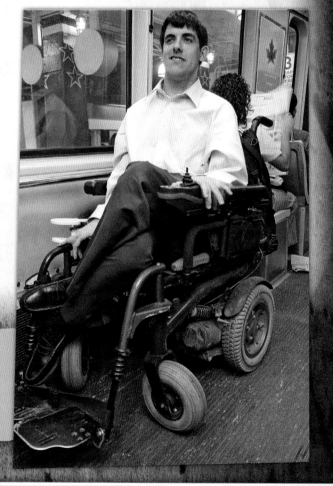

A person with cerebral palsy may need to use a wheelchair to get around.

Case study

As much as Joshua loves to play sports, sometimes it gets frustrating for him because of his asthma. Sometimes when he runs, he feels like it's a struggle between him and his breath. He says that he just focuses on the finish line and sprints, knowing that the end is just a few strides away. Excitement and pride fill Joshua when he crosses the finish line.

Changes

Chronic illness often requires lifestyle changes. Sometimes changes in daily **routine** are required. A person who has an illness that limits physical movement may need to use a wheelchair to get around. Someone who has an illness that affects digestion may need to avoid certain foods or change his or her diet.

Sometimes having a chronic illness limits a person's ability to lead a normal life. A person with a chronic illness may tire easily and need to rest more often than other people. Even if a person has a chronic illness that will last a lifetime, this doesn't mean that he or she can't enjoy life. But it does often mean that taking medicine or **adjusting** their lifestyle may be necessary to fight the illness.

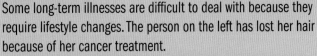

Some long-term illnesses are difficult to deal with because they require lifestyle changes. The person on the left has lost her hair because of her cancer treatment.

Childhood and adult illnesses

Childhood illnesses

Some illnesses affect children more often than adults. It is difficult to be young and be sick. It is not fun to be tired, in pain, or in a bad mood.

Many children get ear infections. Germs can get into a person's ear and an infection starts to grow. Chicken pox is another common childhood illness. It is caused by a virus. Chicken pox is very contagious and causes red, itchy spots to appear on the body. It can be spread quickly to many other children. Sometimes adults can get chicken pox, too.

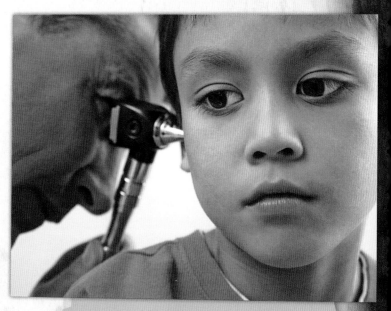

Most people will get at least one ear infection during childhood.

Many childhood illnesses are common illnesses that last a short amount of time, for example one or two weeks. But other childhood illnesses are more serious.

NEWSFLASH

People who live in a house where someone smokes are called passive smokers. This means these people are not smoking, but they are still breathing in the smoke. Passive smokers may have an increased risk of ear infections, chronic coughs, and asthma.

Adult illnesses

There are some illnesses that happen more often in adults. When a parent is ill, a child can feel sad. It can be a scary time for the whole family. Talking and sharing feelings can help everyone feel better.

There are some cancers that happen in both adults and children, but colon cancer and breast cancer are two types of cancers that mainly happen in adults. **Alzheimer's disease** is an illness that affects the brain. People with this illness have problems with their memory. As they grow older, they lose the ability to remember family and friends and how to do simple everyday tasks.

There is currently no cure for Alzheimer's disease, but scientists are working hard to find one.

There are many illnesses that affect both children and adults. Both children and adults should visit the doctor when they are sick. Everyone should lead a healthy lifestyle by exercising and eating sensibly to avoid preventable illnesses.

Case study

When Molly's grandpa had Alzheimer's disease, he forgot how to read the newspaper or even a picture book. He did remember a lot of things that happened when he was a little boy. Molly loved to listen to his stories about his childhood in Holland.

Some people are born with an illness.

Why do illnesses happen?

Illnesses can happen in babies, children, and adults. Sometimes there is a specific cause of an illness, but other times there is no reason why a person gets an illness.

Born with an illness

Sometimes babies are born with an illness. For parents and family, this can be a very scary time. Seeing a baby in the hospital can be difficult.

Inherited illness

Some people **inherit** illnesses from their family. An inherited illness is caused when a **gene** is passed from the parent to the child. This gene carries the information that causes the illness.

An inherited illness is sometimes discovered as soon as a baby is born. Other times, people do not find out that they have an inherited illness until later on, when they are teenagers or even adults.

NEWSFLASH

Genes are what makes a person special. They determine a person's physical features, such as the colour of a person's eyes, the size of a person's nose, and if a person is a girl or boy. Doctors are working with genes to learn more about illnesses.

Environmental causes

Some chronic illnesses are caused by the **environment**. Pesticides, household cleaners, and smog have all been connected with chronic illnesses in people. Asthma and other respiratory illnesses can be caused by air pollution and harmful working conditions.

Scientists and doctors study groups of people who have the same illnesses to learn what causes people to get sick. Doctors have learned that smoking can cause lung cancer. People who smoke or are around smokers can be harmed by the smoke they breathe in.

Living with an illness caused by the environment can be very frustrating. Sometimes people may feel angry at the world. Living in a certain place can make environmentally caused illnesses worse.

Some illnesses are caused or made worse by environmental factors, such as pollution. This photograph shows air pollution over Los Angeles, USA.

No reason

Some illnesses just happen. Often doctors don't know what causes these illnesses or why they occur in certain people. It can be hard to deal with an illness that doesn't have a known cause. But all illnesses, whether discovered at birth, inherited, caused by the environment, or without a known cause, can be difficult to live with.

Diagnosis

Going to the doctor

When people are very ill, they call the doctor's office for an appointment. People go to the doctor to find out what is wrong. Many people get nervous when it is time to go to the doctor. Asking questions about what will happen during the visit can help make a person feel better about the actual visit. People who have to go to the doctor may need to miss school or other activities.

To make a **diagnosis**, the doctor will need to perform a physical examination and order tests to be done on the patient. Sometimes waiting for the test results can take days or weeks. Sometimes a person will need to go to several doctors before the problem is discovered. Waiting for test results can be difficult, especially when you are not feeling well.

When the doctor has all the test results and knows what is wrong, he or she can make a diagnosis. Doctors study for many years to learn ways to diagnose illnesses.

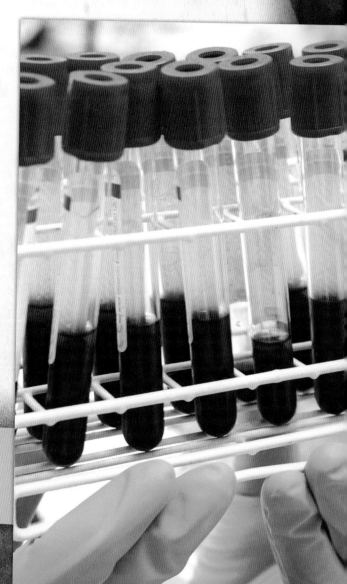

Doctors can order different blood tests to help make a diagnosis.

An MRI (magnetic resonance imaging) machine is one of the best and newest tools for diagnosing many illnesses. MRI uses radio waves and a strong magnetic field to look at the inside of a person's body. An MRI makes a clunking noise as it passes over a body part to take a picture.

Doctors can find out many things by looking at a person's MRI images.

Tools used in diagnosis

Today, medical experts have more tools for diagnosing illnesses than ever before. Blood tests, x-rays, and body **scans** are just a few of the many different tools available to doctors. Tests can be done in doctors' offices, labs, hospitals, and other places. It can be scary to go for any type of medical test. People who are upset or nervous about tests should talk to their family. It is important to remember that medical tests help discover why a person isn't feeling well.

Test results can tell a doctor what is going on inside the body. Doctors learn how different body parts are working together from tests. Another way for the doctor to learn how the body is working is to ask questions and listen to the patient. A patient who answers the questions honestly is helpful to the doctor.

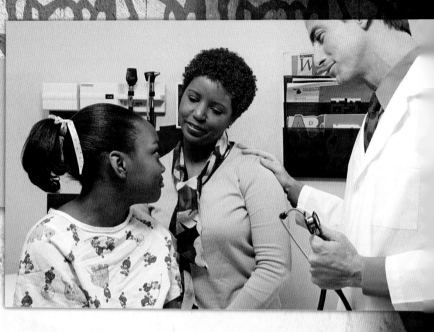

Being diagnosed with an illness is often a confusing time in a person's life.

Hearing the diagnosis

When all of the person's information and test results are gathered, the doctor can tell the patient what the diagnosis is. Hearing the diagnosis can be frightening. People are often nervous, worried, or relieved when they hear a diagnosis.

Having a variety of different feelings about diagnosis is normal. A person can be scared or anxious when they don't know what will happen next. A person can feel relieved to finally know what the illness is and start treatment. Often young people do not understand all the medical terms used. Teenagers should always ask questions or say that they don't understand what something is or what something means.

Doctors and nurses can give support and help calm any fears the patient and their family may have by answering questions and explaining what will happen next.

Case study

Amanda tried to be brave when she heard the news that she had cancer. She felt that the doctor was good at telling her about the disease and what to expect. The only thing that really got to her was when the doctor said Amanda would lose her hair.

Dealing with the diagnosis

All people are different, and each person **copes** with an illness his or her own way. Some people want to know everything there is to know about their illness. They ask questions and learn about the illness. Knowledge gives some people control over their illness. Other people can only handle a little information at a time. Some people want to share the news of their illness, while others want to keep the diagnosis private.

Open and honest communication is best when living with a person who has an illness. It is okay to ask questions like, "Are you in pain?" or "Is there anything I can I do to help you?". Asking questions gives people a chance to talk about their illness. Family members who talk and share their feelings can more easily solve problems and support each other.

NEWSFLASH

Over a million children and young people in the United Kingdom have asthma. That is more than the entire population of the city of Leeds.

It is normal to have a variety of feelings, such as sadness or fear, after being diagnosed with an illness.

Treatment and care

Different types of treatment

Each illness is different and requires its own plan for treatment. After doctors make a diagnosis, they come up with a plan. The medical team explains all the options available for the patient's illness. Most illnesses require some treatment.

Many different people can be involved in the treatment plan. **Physical therapists** and **counsellors** can help answer questions and calm any fears a person may have. Doctor, patient, and family all need to discuss options for treatment and work together for the best outcome of an illness.

Taking medicine is a common treatment for illness. Medicine can be picked up at a chemists.

Medicines

Medicines can be one form of treatment for illnesses. Medicines come in many different forms such as pills, liquids, ointments, and lotions. People who must take medicine should follow the directions carefully. It is important to remember that taking medicine correctly helps in handling an illness.

Medicines can have different **side effects** on people. A headache, rash, or stomachache can be side effects of some medicines. When people have questions about their medicine, they can ask a chemist. Chemists are trained to explain what medicines can do.

Surgery and hospital visits

Some illnesses require the patient to go to the hospital. Being in the hospital can be a scary experience. Lying in a strange bed, being poked, and getting examined can be difficult. Some hospital stays are short, while others are much longer.

Some illnesses require a hospital stay for an operation or other treatment method, such as **chemotherapy**. Hospital procedures can be frightening, even for an adult.

There are medical people in the hospital that can answer questions about operations and other procedures. Doctors, nurses, and other hospital staff all work together to help patients get better.

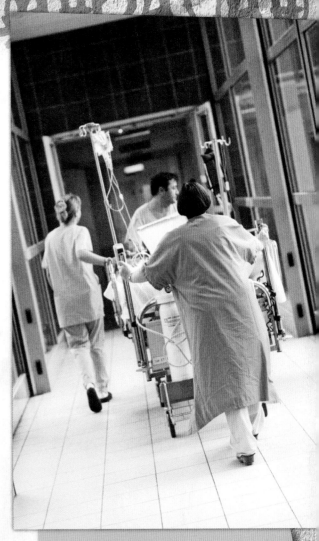

Surgery is sometimes necessary to help cure some illnesses.

Top tips

Here are some tips for the most effective treatment:

- Go to all scheduled doctor appointments.
- Take all medicine on time.
- Ask questions and stay involved in treatment plans and options.
- Talk with an adult about feelings and fears.

Handling changes

Many major illnesses require treatments that change a person's lifestyle. Treatments sometimes interfere with a person's daily routine. A person may not be able to go out for break times, but maybe some friends can stay in and play a game. A special event or activity like a sleepover at a friend's house may need to wait until the person is feeling better. It can be hard to cope with the changes that an illness brings.

People being treated for an illness sometimes feel like they are not in control of their life. Feelings of frustration, anger, and being different, are normal reactions. Sometimes people feel disappointed in their bodies.

Certain illnesses can be treated without going to the hospital. Some people who have diabetes can give themselves insulin shots to help control their illness.

You can control certain parts of your life by making good food choices.

The teenage years are a period of time when young people want to be more independent. Young people can't imagine their bodies not working the way they should. Teenagers with an illness find it difficult to be dependent on others for help. They also struggle with illness because they realize how serious some illnesses can be, they fear being different from friends, and they worry about being left out of activities.

Making choices

It is important for young people to remember that they can make choices and be involved in their treatment. For example, people with diabetes can make choices about what foods they are going to eat for each meal. They can check their own blood sugar levels and give themselves **insulin**. People with asthma can learn more about how their medicines work and how to use them to have the best effect on their breathing. They can also learn how much activity they can safely do and when to rest.

What do you think?

Some people think patients should follow only the doctor's treatment plan. Modern medicine has been shown to be effective and safe. Other people think patients should be allowed to explore and choose different methods of treatment as well, such as special diets. What do you think about alternative treatment plans?

Coping with major illness

Some illnesses are more serious than others. It can be very hard to cope with illnesses that require lifestyle changes.

Time away from home

Sometimes people with an illness need to be away from home for treatment. Being away from home is difficult for the whole family. The person who is ill misses his or her family and friends, and family and friends miss the person who is ill.

Nothing seems normal when someone is missing from the family. Family members have their own duties and responsibilities, but when one person is away people often feel the need to pick up more responsibilities. This can cause **stress**. Young people sometimes feel they need to grow up and help out. But even when a parent is ill, children and teenagers still need to go to school and go out with their friends.

Case study

When Kelly is sick and needs to go to the hospital, she misses her friends, and even her teachers. One time when she was at the hospital, her class at school had a holiday party. Kelly was sad about missing the party. She says that she sometimes feels that it is very unfair to be sick.

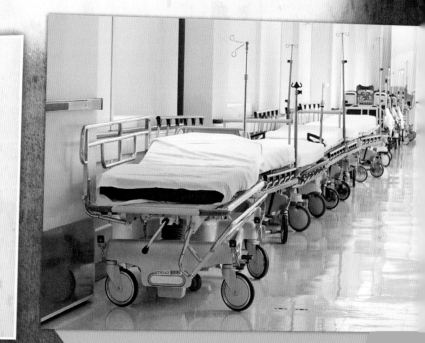

Being in hospital can be stressful. Hospitals are full of unfamiliar objects and equipment.

It is important for patients to tell their doctor or nurse how they are feeling.

Hospital stays

Staying at a hospital can be a frightening experience. It is important to remember that workers at the hospital want to help patients get better. People who are ill may go to the hospital for tests, treatments, or surgeries. Parents are often allowed to stay overnight with their child.

While in the hospital, a patient may feel like there is no time to rest. A hospital can be a very busy place. When the tests or other activities are finished, hospitals have activities a person can do to take his or her mind off the illness. Patients can watch television, read a book from the hospital library, or listen to music. Keeping a diary or writing poetry sometimes helps a person to express feelings. Some hospitals have a play room where patients can go to get out of their room.

The whole family

Some patients and families feel like their world has turned upside down when they hear a diagnosis. When one person has an illness, the whole family needs to learn how to cope with that illness. When a family member is ill, routines may need to change.

Brothers or sisters can have many feelings when a sibling is ill. They can feel guilty or frightened. Sometimes they worry they may get sick too. These feelings are all normal. It is important to share feelings and thoughts with other family members.

Talking to family or friends can help you cope with an illness.

Case study

Paul said that he was so scared when he found out that his brother had cancer. He said that cancer always seemed so terrible in films. Then Paul realized that he didn't really know that much about cancer. He started reading and learned a lot. He found out that most children survive cancer.

Communication is not always verbal. Art can be a helpful way to express feelings and fears.

Missing school and activities

Sometimes people who are ill need to stay home and miss school. Teachers can send home schoolwork and talk with the pupil to come up with a plan for the pupil to catch up. Being ill can mean missing social events. Friends are especially important during teenage years and being ill, missing friends, and not being able to do things you want to can be very difficult. Feelings of frustration, being left out, and being alone are important to share with other people.

Appearance changes

When some people are ill, their appearance can change. They can lose weight, lose their hair, or have to wear bandages. Fears of looking different, people staring, and wondering what others are thinking are all experiences people with illnesses have. Most people understand that people being treated for an illness may not look like their usual self.

NEWSFLASH

Recent studies have shown that working on an art project helps to lessen pain, reduce tiredness, and improve appetite in patients. Art allows patients to think about something other than their illness and gives them something they can control.

Getting help

Being ill is not easy. Having an illness is a time for family and friends to be together and help each other. Other people can also help during a time of illness. Doctors, counsellors, religious groups, and support groups are ready to help patients and their families.

Many people find that spending time with family and friends helps them feel better. People who are ill need to find what works best for them.

Research shows laughter is one of the best ways to release stress.

What do you think?

Some people think being around, talking to, and sharing with people who have the same illness is helpful. Other people think it is too hard to be around other sick people. What do you think?

An illness may mean many changes, but it can also be a time to get closer to family and friends.

It is important to remember that illness is tough to deal with. Ways to remain strong are to keep a positive attitude, learn about the illness, and talk about the illness with an adult. Share your thoughts, feelings, and fears with others. Communication is important when there is someone ill in the family. Adults can help talk about feelings and concerns.

It can be very hard to have any type of illness, or to have a family member or friend who has an illness. Being diagnosed and receiving proper treatment are the first steps to getting an illness under control. People living with an illness often have good days and bad days. Remember to keep a positive attitude during both.

Facts about illness

- Germs are so small that they can only be seen with a microscope.

- The common cold can be caused by one of more than 200 different viruses.

- Each year more than 10,000 young people learn their brother or sister has been diagnosed with cancer.

- Diabetes is one of the most common chronic illnesses in school-aged children.

- Alcohol and recreational drugs can be deadly to teenagers with chronic illnesses.

- Some medicines, called sublingual, are placed under the tongue and are absorbed through blood vessels and into the bloodstream.

- Becoming informed about illnesses can help lessen fears.

- Keeping a positive attitude through an illness will help a person to cope better.

Glossary

adjust get used to a change

Alzheimer's disease disease that affects the brain and causes forgetfulness and loss of ability to do everyday things

arthritis condition that affects the joints and causes moving difficulties

asthma illness that affects the lungs and causes breathing problems

cancer illness where cells grow out of control, clump together to form tumours, and destroy normal healthy cells

cerebral palsy condition that affects the muscles and the way the body moves

chemotherapy type of treatment used to fight cancer

chronic something that is always present and does not go away

cope deal with

counsellor someone who is trained to help people with their problems

Crohn's disease disease that affects digestion, the colon, and the bowel

cystic fibrosis disease that affects the lungs and the digestive system

diabetes disease that affects the body's ability to use energy from food

diagnosis identifying an illness or condition

environment everything around us, conditions that surround a person

gene part of a cell in the body that has instructions about growth and development

germ tiny organism that can cause illness

heart disease illness or condition affecting the heart

inhaler device used to breathe medicine in through the mouth

inherit receive something from someone

insulin hormone that converts sugar, starches, and other food into energy needed for daily life

isolated alone

physical therapist someone who is trained to help people improve their health or recover from an injury or illness

routine usual habits and way of life

scan picture of the inside of the body made by a machine

side effect unwanted thing that happens besides the intended effect

stress worry, strain, or pressure

virus tiny organism that can grow inside living cells to cause illness

Further resources

Illness is difficult to deal with. If you or someone you know has an illness, remember that you aren't alone. As well as your family and friends, there are many resources available to help you cope with an illness.

Books

Just the Facts: Cancer, Oliver Gillie (Heinemann Library, 2004)

Just the Facts: Diabetes, Jenny Bryan (Heinemann Library, 2004)

What Does it Mean to Have Asthma?, Louise Spilsbury (Heinemann Library, 2001)

What Does it Mean to Have Sickle Cell Anaemia?, Louise Spilsbury (Heinemann Library, 2001)

Websites

Childline
www.childline.org.uk/ContactChildLine.asp
Contact details for Childline are on this page. They can help with whatever problems you may have.

Diabetes
www.diabetes.org.uk/Guide-to-diabetes/My-life/Teens/
This site is for older children but contains some useful information about what happens when you discover you have diabetes. It also has a help and support section.

Make-a-wish
www.make-a-wish.org.uk/
The Make-A-Wish Foundation grants the wishes of young people who have life-threatening medical conditions.

Other people's experiences
www.click4tic.org.uk/Home
This site allows you to read about other young people who have or have had major diseases.

Organizations

There are many organizations that help people with different types of illnesses. The following organizations have helpful websites that include information on a particular illness, as well as advice for dealing with that particular illness. If the illness that you are looking for isn't listed below, ask an adult to help you find information.

ACT (Association for Children's Palliative Care)
Orchard House
Orchard Lane
Bristol BS1 5DT
Tel: 0117 922 1556
www.act.org.uk
ACT is the association for children with life-threatening or terminal conditions and their families. They provide information about support services for families whose children have life-threatening or terminal illnesses.

Cancer Research UK
P.O. Box 123
London WC2A 3PX
Tel: 020 7061 8355
www.cancerresearchuk.org
Cancer Research UK is the biggest cancer research organization outside the United States. It funds research and develops drugs to help fight cancer. If you have a question about cancer then you can call the number above. They also have a number of leaflets that can help you learn more about the disease.

Diabetes UK Central Office
Macleod House,
10 Parkway
London NW1 7AA
Tel: 020 7424 1000
www.diabetes.org.uk/
This organization provides information to help teenagers and their families find out about all diabetes.

Index